Questions and Answers: Countries

# Vietnam

A Question and Answer Book

by Mary Englar

Consultant:
Christoph Giebel, Associate Professor
International Studies/History
University of Washington at Seattle

Capstone
press
Mankato, Minnesota

Fact Finders is published by Capstone Press
151 Good Counsel Drive, P.O. Box 669, Mankato, Minnesota 56002.
www.capstonepress.com

*Library of Congress Cataloging-in-Publication Data*
Englar, Mary.
    Vietnam: a question and answer book / by Mary Englar.
    p. cm.—(Fact finders. Questions and answers. Countries)
    Includes bibliographical references (p. 31) and index.
    Summary: "Describes the geography, history, economy, and culture of Vietnam in a question-and-answer format"—Provided by publisher.
    ISBN–13: 978–0–7368–6414–5 (hardcover)
    ISBN–10: 0–7368–6414–8 (hardcover)
    1. Vietnam—Miscellanea—Juvenile literature. I. Title. II. Series.
DS556.3.E54 2007
959.7—dc22                                                                2006005060

**Editorial Credits**
Silver Editions, editorial, design, and production; Kia Adams, set designer; Ortelius Design, Inc., cartographer; Wanda Winch, photo researcher; Scott Thoms, photo editor

**Photo Credits**
Art Directors/Andrew Gasson, 13; Capstone Press/Karon Dubke, 24; Corbis/Bettmann, 7; Corbis/Chris Lisle, cover (background), 11; Corbis/Free Agents Limited, 20; Corbis/John R. Jones; Papilio, 21; Cory Langley, 1; Getty Images Inc./AFP/Hoang Dinh Nam, 9, 19; Getty Images Inc./AFP/STR, 23; Getty Images Inc./Bongarts/Alexander Hassenstein, 18; Getty Images Inc./Iconica/Frans Lemmens, 8; Getty Images Inc./Stone/Erica Lansner, 27; Getty Images Inc./The Image Bank/John William Banagan, 4; Index Stock Imagery/Fred Scribner, cover (foreground); Photo Courtesy of Paul Baker, 29 (coins); Peter Arnold/Jorgen Schytte, 15, 17, 25; Photodisc, 29 (flag); Photo Courtesy of Richard Sutherland, 29 (bill); SuperStock/Steve Vidler, 12

1 2 3 4 5 6 11 10 09 08 07 06

# Table of Contents

## Features

# Where is Vietnam?

Vietnam is in Southeast Asia. It is a little larger than the U.S. state of New Mexico.

Vietnam is long and narrow. Its coastline is 2,140 miles (3,444 kilometers) long. Near Vietnam's center, only 30 miles (48 kilometers) separate the sea from Laos.

*Plentiful rivers make boat travel in the Mekong Delta easy.*

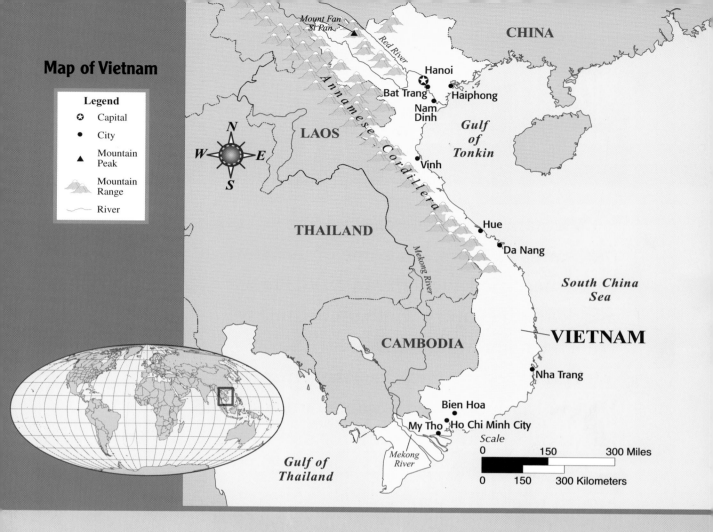

Map of Vietnam

**Legend**

| | |
|---|---|
| ✪ | Capital |
| ● | City |
| ▲ | Mountain Peak |
| | Mountain Range |
| | River |

Mountains and **plateaus** cover much of Vietnam. Low areas are found near the Red and Mekong rivers.

Temperatures are cooler in the north than in the south. In both areas, **monsoon** winds bring heavy rain every summer.

# When did Vietnam become a country?

Vietnam has been a country for thousands of years. For some of that time, China **occupied** Vietnam. In 1858, France attacked the country. Vietnam became a French colony in the 1860s.

The Vietnamese wanted their freedom. Ho Chi Minh declared independence in 1945. His army fought the French for nine years. In 1954, the French and the Vietnamese agreed to end the war.

## Fact!

*The United States fought alongside Saigon against Hanoi from 1961 until 1973. After the war, the U.S. cut all ties with Vietnam for almost 20 years.*

*Ho Chi Minh, shown here in 1958, led the Vietnamese in their fight for freedom from the French.*

By then, Ho Chi Minh's government in Hanoi, in North Vietnam, was opposed by another government in Saigon, in South Vietnam. Both governments wanted to rule all of Vietnam. In 1975, after many years of fighting, the Hanoi government and its supporters won.

# What type of government does Vietnam have?

Vietnam has a **communist** government. In the past, the government owned all the land and factories. Today, many people own land, businesses, and houses.

Vietnam's elections are different from those in the United States. All candidates are supportive of the Communist Party. Everyone 18 years old or older can vote.

## Fact!

*The body of Ho Chi Minh (1890–1969) was preserved after he died. He was the first president of the Democratic Republic of Vietnam, which later became the central government. Visitors to Hanoi can view his body in its glass coffin.*

*Prime Minister Phan Van Khai gives a speech to the National Assembly in 2005.*

Every five years, the people elect members of the National Assembly. These lawmakers choose one member to be president. The president represents Vietnam in other countries and oversees the military. The president appoints a prime minister to manage the government.

# What kind of housing does Vietnam have?

Most Vietnamese live in small towns and villages. Their houses often have bamboo pole, wood, or concrete frames. Roofs are made with palm leaves, metal, or tile.

Most houses have only two or three rooms. Families eat in the main room. The smaller rooms are bedrooms.

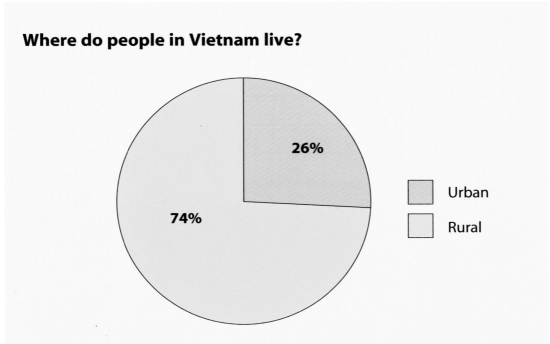

**Where do people in Vietnam live?**

26%

74%

Urban

Rural

*Most people in the Mekong Delta fish to earn a living. Homes are often built right on the edge of the river.*

Vietnam's cities are very crowded. Most people live in apartments. Modern apartments and houses are built with concrete walls. Some wealthy families build large homes with two or three stories.

11

# What are Vietnam's forms of transportation?

Vietnam's cities have modern, crowded roads. Still, most Vietnamese do not own cars. They take motorcycle taxis, minibuses, and bicycles to work.

For long-distance trips, there are other options. Planes fly between major cities. A train runs between Ho Chi Minh City in the south to Hanoi in the north. This trip takes 34 hours.

## Fact!

*A popular form of city transportation is a three-wheeled bicycle taxi called a cyclo. It has a seat in the front. The driver pedals his customers wherever they want to go.*

*Bicycles, cars, and people on foot all crowd a busy street in Ho Chi Minh City.*

In the country, transportation is simpler. People pull carts behind their bicycles. Some children ride water buffalos to the market. The Mekong and Red River deltas have many rivers and canals. People use boats to take animals and food to the market.

# What are Vietnam's major industries?

More than 60 percent of Vietnamese are farmers. They grow rice, coffee, corn, and sugar cane. Vietnam is one of the largest exporters of rice in the world.

Most farms in Vietnam are small. Farmers grow enough food for their families. Many farmers also raise ducks and chickens for extra money.

## What does Vietnam import and export?

| Imports | Exports |
|---|---|
| machinery | oil |
| equipment | seafood |
| oil | rice |
| fertilizer | coffee |
| steel | rubber |
| cotton | tea |

*Vietnamese wear cone hats to protect themselves from the sun while working in the rice fields.*

Other Vietnamese work in manufacturing and services. Factories make shoes and clothing. Others process seafood and coffee. Hotels employ many service workers. Tourists come for the beautiful beaches and to see rare animals such as tigers and rhinos.

# What is school like in Vietnam?

Primary schools in Vietnam are free for all children. In small villages, schools often have only one room. Classes often have 50 students. Students wear uniforms of dark pants and a white shirt. Some wear red scarves around their necks.

Students go to school from September until May. They attend school Monday through Saturday. Most students go to school for half a day.

## Fact!

*Some students in Vietnam's mountains speak Mon-Khmer or Malayo-Polynesian at home. When they start school, they must learn Vietnamese to understand the lessons.*

*Students share tables in a primary school classroom.*

Vietnam does not have enough schools, supplies, or teachers for all its students. In the mountains, one school will often serve a large area. Students may walk many miles to school each day.

# What are Vietnam's favorite sports and games?

Soccer is the most popular sport in Vietnam. National teams play against other Asian teams for a chance to play in the World Cup. Children often play soccer in parks and on city streets.

Many individual sports are also popular. People of all ages play badminton and table tennis. Martial arts such as karate and tae kwon do are also popular with girls and boys.

## Fact!

*In 2000, Vietnam won its first Olympic medal. Tran Hieu Ngan won a silver medal in Women's Tae Kwon Do.*

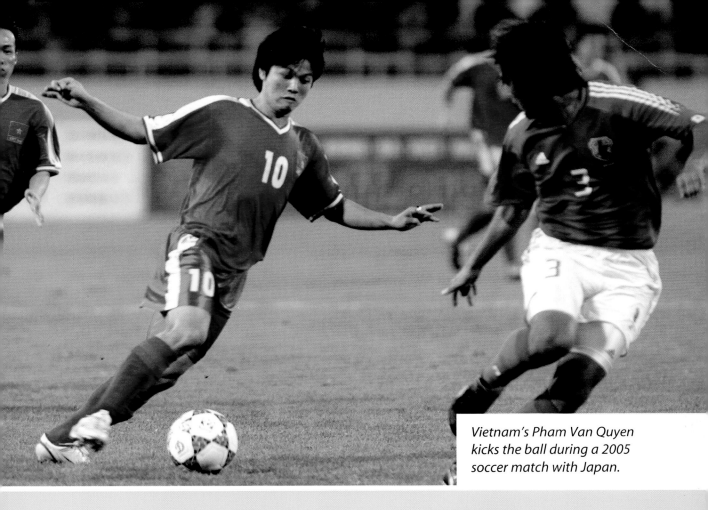

*Vietnam's Pham Van Quyen kicks the ball during a 2005 soccer match with Japan.*

Every year, Vietnam has a national sports festival in August. Students from all over Vietnam play for medals in a variety of sports. Events include soccer, wrestling, badminton, and martial arts.

# What are the traditional art forms in Vietnam?

Vietnam is known for its crafts. In villages near Hanoi, artists make pottery, metal crafts, and jewelry. Families pass the traditions down to their children.

In Bat Trang, potters make dishes, flower vases, and pots with traditional designs. Artists paint dragons, turtles, tigers, and landscapes on the pots.

## Fact!

*Water puppets are unique to Vietnam. The puppeteers stand waist deep in water behind a screen. The puppeteers make the puppets appear to dance on the water.*

*A Vietnamese artist paints a design on a large ceramic vase.*

Farmers in central Vietnam raise silkworms. The silkworms are fed mulberry leaves. When they are fully grown, the worms spin a cocoon of silk thread. The farmers then heat the cocoons and unravel the thread. Silk is made into fabric for clothing and other goods.

# What holidays do people in Vietnam celebrate?

Many Vietnamese holidays are celebrated on the **lunar calendar**. The most important holiday is Tet. Tet falls on the first new moon of the year. The celebration lasts three days.

During Tet, families say prayers for their dead **ancestors**. Relatives give children money in red envelopes. Everyone wears his or her best clothes. One favorite Tet food is a cake made from sticky rice.

## What other holidays do people in Vietnam celebrate?

*New Year's Day*
*May Day*
*Ho Chi Minh's Birthday*
*Independence Day*

*Elephants kneel down to greet the audience at the beginning of the Elephant Race Festival.*

In the highlands, the Elephant Race Festival is held in the spring. Riders race their elephants for about 1 mile (1.6 kilometers). People bang drums and cheer for the elephants. The winning elephant receives sugar cane.

# What are the traditional foods of Vietnam?

The Vietnamese eat rice with every meal. Rice is mixed with vegetables and bits of chicken.

*Pho* is a famous noodle soup in Vietnam. *Pho* is made with beef or chicken. Some Vietnamese eat it for breakfast. Hungry customers buy *pho* from street stands any time of the day or evening.

## Fact!

Nuoc Mam *is a fish sauce served with every meal. It takes four to 12 months to make the fish sauce. The smell is so strong that Vietnam Airlines does not allow any fish sauce on its flights.*

*Vietnamese use chopsticks
to eat most of their meals.*

At mealtime, bowls filled with food
are placed in the center of the table. Every
person has a rice bowl for their meal. People
take food from the dishes with chopsticks.
Everyone takes only what they want, and
nothing goes to waste.

# What is family life like in Vietnam?

Parents, grandparents, and children live together in the country. Everyone helps with the crops and animals.

Farmers do not make much money. Many young people leave the country to find jobs. They often work in factories or drive taxis in the cities.

**What are the ethnic backgrounds of people in Vietnam?**

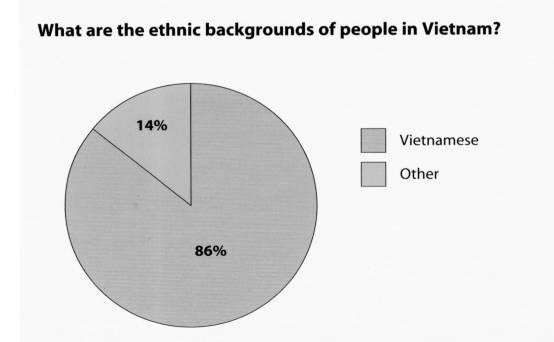

14%

86%

Vietnamese

Other

*A man leads his son on a water buffalo in the countryside near Hanoi.*

City life can be crowded and busy. A large extended family might share one apartment. Many Vietnamese have two jobs. Sometimes children help their parents in their shops or restaurants.

# Vietnam Fast Facts

**Official name:**

Socialist Republic of Vietnam

**Land area:**

125,622 square miles
(325,360 square kilometers)

**Average annual precipitation:**

63 inches (161 centimeters)

**Average January temperature (Hanoi):**

59 degrees Fahrenheit
(15 degrees Celsius)

**Average July temperature (Hanoi):**

86 degrees Fahrenheit
(30 degrees Celsius)

**Population:**

83,535,576 people

**Capital city:**

Hanoi

**Languages:**

Vietnamese (Official), English,
Chinese, Khmer, and more than
50 others

**Natural resources:**

Phosphates, coal, copper, silver,
gold, oil, gas, forests

**Religions:**

| No religion | 80.8% |
| Buddhist | 9.3% |
| Catholic | 6.7% |
| Protestant | .5% |
| Other | 2.7% |

# Money and Flag

## Money:

*Vietnamese money is called the dong. In 2006, one U.S. dollar equaled 15,912 dong. One Canadian dollar equaled 13,811 dong.*

## Flag:

*The Vietnamese flag has a yellow star on a red background. Red represents the blood of the soldiers who fought for independence. The star represents workers, farmers, soldiers, teachers, and young people working together.*

29

# Learn to Speak Vietnamese

Most people in Vietnam speak Vietnamese. It is Vietnam's official language. Learn to speak some Vietnamese words.

| English | Vietnamese | Pronunciation |
|---------|-----------|---------------|
| hello | xin chao | SIN CHOW |
| good-bye | chao | JAU |
| please | lam on | LAHM UHN |
| thank you | cam on | KAHM UHN |
| yes | vang | vah-UHNG |
| yes (south) | da | YAH |
| no | khong | kah-OHNG |
| My name is | ten toi la | TAIN TOY LAH |

# Glossary

ancestor (AN-sess-tur)—a member of a family that lived a long time ago

communist (KOM-yuh-nihst)—relating to communism; communism is a way of organizing a country so the land, houses, and businesses are owned by all but administered by the government.

lunar calendar (LOO-nur KAL-uhn-dur)—a calendar that follows the cycles of the moon traveling around earth

monsoon (mon-SOON)—strong winds that blow from the ocean to the land, bringing heavy rain

occupied (OK-yuh-pyed)—when an army takes over and controls another country

plateau (pla-TOH)—an area of high, flat land

# Internet Sites

FactHound offers a safe, fun way to find Internet sites related to this book. All of the sites on FactHound have been researched by our staff.

Here's how:
1. Visit *www.facthound.com*
2. Choose your grade level.
3. Type in this book ID **0736864148** for age-appropriate sites. You may also browse subjects by clicking on letters, or by clicking on pictures and words.
4. Click on the **Fetch It** button.

FactHound will fetch the best sites for you!

# Read More

**De Capua, Sarah E.** *Vietnam*. First Reports. Minneapolis: Compass Point Books, 2003.

**Gray, Shirley Wimbish.** *Vietnam*. A True Book. New York: Children's Press, 2003.

**Morgan, Tom.** *In a Vietnamese City*. A Child's Day. New York: Benchmark Books, 2002.

**Ng, Yumi and Amy Condra-Peters.** *Welcome to Vietnam*. Welcome to My Country. Milwaukee, Wisc.: Gareth Stevens, 2003.

# Index